THE

LITTLE

COOKBOOK

OF

PHILOSOPHY

BY KEITH EMERLING

With so many small stores and local purveyors,
I have decided to leave out a reference section.
Please support local agriculture and shopkeepers
whenever possible. If it becomes necessary to source
ingredients online you can use a search engine
term like "buy [ingredient]."

Thanks to the recipe testers:

Julia Erickson, Lee Everett, Kas Maroney,
Donna Massery, Wendy Wray Miller, Emily Paskus,
Robin Schmitt, Carrie Wright.

Additional recipe testers include:
Diane Firtell, Arlene Murdock,
Donna Todd Rivers

Thanks to Emily Banner for help refining
the content and to Bess Hochstein for
editorial assistance.

Content created on iPhone 5s.
Layout and revisions via Adobe InDesign on desktop.

Thank you to Kimberly Donoughe for design support.

CONSIDERING THE TRANSITORY NATURE OF FOOD

Food follows a long and circuitous path. Farmers grow it. We work to get the money to buy it. The money travels in our wallets to the store. We transport food from its origin, to the place of purchase and to the location where we prepare and consume it. Food then travels through the process of digestion and the cycle of human nutrition to provide sustenance. Thinking more about where food comes from and more fully appreciating this cycle can bring a beautiful responsibility to an already enriching experience.

Eating is a significant act. We cannot survive without food. Food links us to parts of our primal physiology. Not only does food support our health and well-being, it also fulfills us in other ways. The act of nourishment also includes cooking. Cooking not only represents an accomplishment in the preparation of the food; it also enriches our participation in acts that define us as a culture and civilization.

Expressing ourselves through cooking satisfies a powerful and basic drive both as a creative act and for the physiological nourishment the meal provides. The fleeting tastes and pleasures of food are an important part of life. It could be said that the fleeting experiences in life define who we are as individuals. Intertwined in sustaining our bodies also lie the nutrients to enrich our lives.

Semolina spaghetti, scallions, sage, sunflower oil, sunflower seeds, sun-dried tomato, sea salt

A vegan dish with foods that begin with the letter "S."

4 bunch scallions, a generous 3/4 lb.

1 bunch fresh sage 1/3 cup

1/3 cup sunflower oil

1/3 cup sunflower seed

2/3 lb. semolina spaghetti

1/3 lb. dried sun-dried tomatoes

sea salt

1/3 cup measure

scale

5 qt. soup pot

food processor and spatula

chef knife and cutting board

4 paper towels or clean dish cloth

Serves 2 to 3 people

1. Toast 1/3 cup raw sunflower seeds in dry soup pot on high heat, tossing seeds continuously. Turn off flame and let seeds continue to toast, tossing seeds more when pan is hottest. When toasted, pour seeds onto clean heat-proof plate. Set aside; let cool.

2. Cut the scallions in two-inch sections; separate white parts from light green and dark green parts. Leave the sage leaves whole.

3. Fill soup pot 1/2 full with water, bring to boil over high heat. Par-boil scallions and sage. First add scallion whites, after 2 minutes add white-ish green parts. After 30 seconds add 1/3 cup fresh sage, leaves only. Cook 30 seconds then add remaining scallion greens and cook for 2 more minutes. Drain in colander and refresh with cold water. Press out excess water in two batches, wrapping in doubled up paper towels or a dish cloth.

4. Add par-boiled scallions and sage to food processor with 1/3 cup sunflower oil. Process into a pesto texture.

5. Refill soup pot until almost full with water and bring to a boil. Cook 2/3 lb. good semolina spaghetti according to instructions.

6. While pasta is cooking julienne 1/3 lb. dried very low salt sun-dried tomatoes.

7. Drain cooked pasta and return to pot. Stir in pesto with 2/3 cups hot water.

8. Add sun-dried tomatoes and sunflower seeds. Mix well and add 1/3 or 2/3 cups more hot water if needed.

9. Add sea salt to taste. Plate and serve immediately, while hot.

VEGAN ALPHABET DINNERS

Make a dinner with 7 ingredients

A
Apricot
Almonds
Avocado
Alfalfa
Adzuki
Ancho
Aubergine

B
Beets
Barley
Butternut
Baguette
Bok Choy
Butterbeans
Brussels sprouts

C
Cabbage
Carrots
Cashew
Caraway
Cauliflower
Curry
Chickpeas
and so on

Millet salad with coarse mustard, maple syrup, maple vinegar and marjoram over braised mustard greens and topped with dried mulberries

Vegan meal made entirely with foods that begin with the letter "M."

mustard greens, 6 to 8 oz. p.p.

1 cup millet

2 Tbsp coarse mustard

1 Tbsp maple syrup

1 Tbsp maple vinegar

1/2 tsp marjoram

mulberries sprinkled to taste

1 cup measure

1 Tbsp measure

1/2 tsp measure

small mixing bowl

2 1/2 qt. sauce pan and lid

12-inch sauté pan

Serves 2-4 people.

1. Add 1 cup hulled millet and 3 cups water to a 2 1/2 qt. sauce pan. Cook covered on medium high heat for 20 minutes, turn off and leave covered.

2. Mix 2 Tbsp coarse mustard, 1 Tbsp maple syrup, 1 Tbsp maple vinegar (or rice vinegar) and 1/2 tsp dried marjoram leaf. Add to millet, mix in and return lid to pan.

3. Add 1/2 cup to 3/4 cup water to a 12-inch sauté pan and place on high heat. Add 3/4 lb. to 1 lb. mustard greens. Turn with tongs and braise until almost all the water is gone.

4. Squeeze out excess moisture with tongs and plate greens. Place millet on top and sprinkle with mulberries. Serve immediately.

Up

What unfolds life in bright ecstasy

Turns forth and endears oneself to reason

Plumes and offerings yet unfurled

Bright and silent cast in beauty

Wonder does one about the presence of self

The bond of Eve and Adam into night

No rib cast or unfurled, truly two

Slip covered, in mind and step

Towards the promise of dream

Waiting in hope of bright future

Lie amongst the stars and chickadee

Singing sweet songs and praise.

Fava beans, fennel, French green beans, fines herbes, filberts & filbert oil, farro, fregola sarda

Vegan farro and fregola salad using foods that begin with the letter "F."

2 lbs. to 2 ½ lbs. fava beans	two 2 ½ qt. sauce pans
1 fennel bulb	3 cup measure
fines herbes:	1 cup measure
2 bunches chive, 1 bunch parsley, ¼ bunch tarragon, 1 bunch chervil	½ cup measure
	colander
½ lb. French green beans (haricots verts)	5 ½ qt. mixing bowl
1 cup raw filberts (hazelnuts)	chef knife & cutting board
½ cup filbert oil (hazelnut oil)	small bowls and plates
1 cup farro	two 1 pint zipper seal plastic bags
1 cup fregola sarda pasta	

Serves 4 to 7 people

1. Toast 1 cup raw hazelnuts in a dry 2 ½ qt. sauce pan. Set aside on a heat-proof plate. When cool place nuts in two 1 pint zipper seal plastic bags and crush. Set aside for topping.

2. In the other sauce pan, toast 1 cup farro and then add 3 cups water and cook 12 to 15 minutes or until done. Drain in colander and set aside on a heat-proof plate.

3. Shell fava beans. In a sauce pan of boiling water, par-boil fava beans for 1 minute. Refresh under cold water and squeeze out of skins. You should have about 1 generous cup. Set aside.

4. Cut the stem ends off ½ lb. of French string beans (*haricots verts*). Cut in into 1-inch sections; you should have 2 cups cut. In a sauce pan of boiling water, par-boil beans until al dente. Refresh under cold water. Set aside in small bowl.

5. Remove outer layer of fennel bulb, if needed, and core it. Slice into julienne strips about 1 inch long. You should have approximately 2 cups raw sliced fennel.

6. Make fresh fines herbes by combining 1 ½ cups sliced chives, ⅓ cup chopped parsley, 1 ½ Tbsp chopped tarragon and 3 Tbsp dried chervil or ¼ cup chopped fresh chervil.

7. Fill one of the sauce pans 2 inches from the top with water, bring to a boil. Add the fregola sarda and cook until almost done. For the last two minutes add the drained farro. For the last minute add the fennel.

8. Place green beans in the bottom of a colander and drain fregola sarda, farro and fennel over the beans.

9. Transfer contents to a 5 ½ qt. mixing bowl and add ½ cup filbert (hazelnut) oil and mix. Add fines herbes and mix, then gently stir in fava beans.

10. Plate and sprinkle the crushed toasted filberts (hazelnuts) on top. Garnish with a fennel frond. Serve while still warm.

Long Shore Drift

I was in one place, now I'm not.

Land looks familiar but it's different.

I foresaw but somehow forgot the spot.

Return is not the same and still here it's exactly not.

Ramp pappardelle with Amish butter, radishes, salt and pepper

The ingredients are the recipe.

EATING

Does one have to kill food with one's bare hands
to honor it enough to eat it?

Does one kill sentient plants to eat them?

Does one just stop eating?

Does one stop living so no one gets hurt?

Can life exist without hurt?

It probably cannot, but life can exist without
excessive or indiscriminate, intentional hurt.

In the case of food, killing something is about as hurtful
as it gets, but death is a part of life. If one chooses life,
one accepts death in the contract of living.

Emotional hurt through difference of opinion
seems unavoidable.

One can strive for a better arrangement with life
and in doing so reduce the amount of hurt inflicted.
The goal is always to cause as little hurt as possible.

Darkling

The end, the near, beginning.
Fear, insight, whole, neglect.
Weary in the way.
Shown shimmer, magnetic.
See start, see bright, see nothing, see light.

Fruit gazpacho: goji berries, green grapes, green figs, golden currants, gooseberries (green & red), golden plum, ginger

A vegan dish with ingredients that begin with the letter "G."

8 oz. dry goji berries (2 cups)	2 cup measure
3/4 lb. green grapes	2 qt. mixing bowl
2 Tbsp tender fresh ginger, chopped	5 qt. mixing bowl
1/2 pint fresh golden currants	food processor
1/2 pint each fresh green and red gooseberries	spatula
1/2 pint green figs	paring knife
3 golden pluot plums	cutting board

Serves 4-6 people.

1. In a 2 qt. mixing bowl soak the dried goji berries in 3 cups cold water for 30 minutes. Scoop out goji berries and add to a food processor with 3/4 lb. green seedless grapes and 2 Tbsp chopped fresh ginger. Purée well. Set aside.

2. While goji berries are soaking, cut up remaining fruit as directed below and place in a in 5 qt. mixing bowl. Reserve some fruit as a garnish.

3. Pluck 1/2 pint golden or blush currants from stem, leave whole. Add to bowl.

4. Cut the tops and tails off the gooseberries. Cut them in half and add to bowl.

5. Cut the top stem from 1/2 pint green figs, cut each fig in 8 pieces. Add to bowl.

6. Cut around pit and add 3 diced golden pluot plums to bowl.

7. Gently toss fresh cut fruit to mix and stir in goji berry, grape and ginger purée.

8. Option: Use the goji berry purée and fruit of your choosing. Other fruits beginning with "G" include: grapefruit, guava, golden raspberries, galia melons, ground cherries, greengage plums, and granny smith, gala, and golden delicious apples.

9. Chill at least 2 hours or until cold and serve in individual bowls with any remaining fruit as a garnish.

Tagliatelle, tomato, trumpet mushroom, tempeh, truffle oil, thyme, Tuscan olive oil XVOO

Vegan pasta, foods beginning with the letter "T."

12 oz. tagliatelle (semolina)

8 oz. tempeh (or more if desired) cut in one inch cubes.

1 pint tomatoes (cherry)

1 ½ cups dried trumpet (black) mushrooms

5 Tbsp Tuscan extra virgin olive oil (XVOO)

½ bunch fresh thyme

3 Tbsp truffle oil (white)

10-inch oven-safe nonstick frying pan

5 qt. soup pot

paring knife

2 qt. mixing bowl

1 ½ cup measure

1 Tbsp measure

salt and pepper to taste

Serves 3-5 people.

1. Preheat oven to 350° F.

2. Add 1 ½ cups dried black trumpet mushrooms to 1 cup water and let soak for 15 minutes or until softened.

3. In a 10-inch oven-safe non-stick frying pan, add enough olive oil to coat the bottom of the pan and place on medium low heat. Add cubed tempeh and fry on two sides until golden brown, about 3 to 5 minutes total. Set aside on a heat-proof plate.

4. Add 1 pint firm cherry tomatoes to the pan and place in preheated oven; roast for 20 to 25 minutes until soft. Set aside.

5. Strip the leaves off ½ bunch of fresh thyme to make 2 Tbsp thyme leaves.

6. Remove softened mushrooms from soaking liquid and sauté briefly in a 5 qt. soup pot. Set aside on a heat-proof plate.

7. Add water to fill 5 qt. soup pot within 1 ½ inches of the top and bring to a boil.

8. While water is reaching a boil, place tempeh on doubled up aluminum foil and place in the oven. Add mushrooms to pan with tomatoes and place in oven. Bake both items approximately ten minutes, or until hot, while you prepare the pasta.

9. Cook 12 oz. semolina tagliatelle according to directions and drain. Return pasta to the empty pot; add 3 Tbsp Tuscan olive oil to pasta with thyme and mix. Salt and pepper to taste.

10. Add tomatoes and mushrooms and mix gently along with 3 Tbsp of white truffle oil.

11. Add tempeh, mix gently and adjust seasoning. Plate and serve immediately.

Sweet potato flour pancake *Lactose and gluten free.*

½ cup sweet potato flour (Peru)

1 ½ tsp baking powder

¾ cup rice milk

2 Tbsp dark brown sugar

3 eggs separated

ghee, grape seed oil or melted coconut oil

4 qt. mixing bowl and whisk for batter

½ cup and ¾ cup measures

1 Tbsp and 1 tsp measures

5 qt. mixing bowl and whisk for egg whites

8-inch to 12-inch fry pan to cook pancakes

flat spatula to flip pancakes

Makes approximately 5 to 8 pancakes

1. In a 4 qt. mixing bowl add ½ cup sweet potato flour, 1 ½ tsp baking powder, ¾ cup rice milk, 2 Tbsp brown sugar, 3 egg yolks and 1 Tbsp melted ghee.

2. Beat egg whites to form medium-stiff peaks, then gently add to the ingredients listed above.

3. Heat a little ghee or oil in the fry pan over medium-low heat, then pour batter into the pan, enough to form 4- to 5-inch pancakes. Flip carefully; they are delicate.

4. Pancakes should be golden brown. Cooking thoroughly helps firm them up. If the recipe is doubled only 5 eggs are needed.

ANIMAL

We are animals not above or below other animals,
we can not deny that is a truth of nature.

'INDUSTRY AND ECONOMICS'

At the management level of the industrial food system, decisions are
made to treat animals in cruel and inhumane ways. Those making the
decisions are often not held accountable for these acts. So often the
animal in its abused state becomes the focus of the conversation, not
the person or people who make the decisions to treat the animals in
this manner. One can see this diversion of attention as a tool to free the
inflictors, of the abuse, from any punishment or responsibility for the
pain they have inflicted.

Like so many things, the animal welfare dynamic does not change
because individual accountability gets outweighed by the huge economic
scale involved. There is just too much cost and profit loss involved in
treating animals humanely. This abuse has been justified by increasing the
efficiency of producing what has now become a product: the meat we
put on the table.

Our industrial food system compromises not only the welfare of animals
but that of the workers, too. The dangerous and unsanitary conditions in
which these animals are being raised is unhealthy for everybody.

This problem is not just confined to raising meat; it is also prevalent in our system of plant-based agriculture, where farm equipment and pesticide use also create dangerous working conditions. Conditions in both forms of food production create tremendous threats to health and well being.

Choosing what you eat is a personal decision, and being responsible in that choice requires attention. Sourcing food in the most humane way possible, vegan or not, is imperative. Being tolerant of other people's food choices also becomes an important part of creating a healthy food system where the abuse of animals and people can be addressed by all.

'Over-easy' goose egg nest: tagliatelle al peperoncino, whole butter, piment D'Espelette, Sarawak pepper, nutmeg and white truffle oil

3oz. tagliatelle al peperoncino dried egg pasta	two 8-inch nonstick fry pans
1/2 Tbsp + 1 Tbsp butter	1 lid for 8-inch fry pan (glass if possible)
2. tsp piment D'Espelette	silicone pasta tongs
1/2 tsp ground Sarawak pepper	1 Tbsp, 1 tsp, 1/2 tsp and 1/4 tsp measures
1/4 tsp heaping grated nutmeg	1 small plate to crack egg into
1/2 tsp sea salt	1 nylon flat spatula to help plate finished dish
1 goose egg or 2 duck eggs or 3 chicken eggs	
1 Tbsp white truffle oil to drizzle	

Serves 1-3 people.

1. On low heat, melt 1/2 Tbsp butter in one of the 8-inch nonstick fry pans to coat bottom. Remove from heat and set aside on an off burner.

2. Mix the nutmeg, pepper, salt and piment D'Espelette in a small dish and set aside.

3. Crack the egg(s) onto a small plate, being careful not to break the yolks. Set aside.

4. Fill the other 8-inch nonstick fry pan 2/3 of way with water and bring to a boil.

5. Immerse the nested egg tagliatelle pasta into the water and cook on high heat scrunching the pasta with the tongs to keep it submerged in the water, approx. 2 to 3 minutes.

6. While pasta is pliable but still a little hard, use tongs on edge of pan to hold the pasta inside the pan and pour out 2/3 of the remaining water. Wipe the pan edge.

7. Return the pan to high heat and reduce liquid until water in the pan is about 1/4 inch deep. Add 1 Tbsp cold butter in one large chunk and sprinkle the dish full of spices over the top.

8. Mix pasta, spices and butter together. Over high heat, reduce the liquid to a thick sauce.

9. When the sauce is thick and reduced, remove pan from heat and add just a few strands of the pasta to the other (now cool) fry pan and make a well in the center of the new pan.

10. Carefully slide the egg(s) into the well. Using the tongs, disperse the whites to cover the bottom of the pan.

11. Using the tongs, carefully arrange the remaining pasta around the yolk until it looks attractive and so the whites set up the around the pasta.

12. Cook with the lid on over medium heat until the egg(s) are done but runny and the whites are set up around the pasta.

13. Carefully slide the pasta out of the pan onto a large dinner plate using the spatula to assist. Drizzle with 1 Tbsp white truffle oil and serve immediately.

'Over-easy' goose egg nest: tagliatelle al peperoncino, whole butter, piment D'Espelette, Sarawak pepper, nutmeg, truffle oil.

Pointillism

*Zen is not about the reaction time in brute force
but seeing the true path of the arrow.*

Kernel

*Control is not about ruling the world,
it is about seeing that the world follows the order of rule.*

Brace

Hate is a convenient excuse not to live your life.

Shaman

*The most important question is the one we ask of
ourselves. Being comfortable with the silence of this
question is a gateway to a more peaceful understanding of
the individual as a person. Being true to this exploration
is a powerful path in a world full of noisiness.*

Sky

There once was a world where a little girl said the sky was orange
and green and purple and pink and from then on no matter what
anyone said, that was the color the sky remained....

Then a little boy looked up at the sky and noticed something quite
odd, the sky never looked anything like what he had been told.

TRANSITION

Are humans at a point where the world we've created moves faster than our ability to process it, so much so, in fact, we no longer understand it or ourselves or how we affect those around us?

Has the concept of "stop" been removed from our "vocabulary"?

Do we know how our electronic devices work? Could we explain and build even an electric toaster or a radio?

Does one default to a primitive part of the brain to essentially exclude information as a natural response to overload? Could this be a hunting/ defense mechanism that allows us to focus on prey or survival?

Could we have transferred this process to people and become an exclusionary society? A society that excludes fellow human beings and the consequence of personal actions rather than just the overload of our surroundings?

Has this form of exclusion shifted to disenfranchisement rather than just physical attack? Do we inflict the hurt through indifference?

The source of our food and the processes it goes through often escape our daily attention. Are we excluding the unpleasantness of this process from our primal urge to eat?

Is there a way to shift our interactions in the world to be more inclusive of differing opinions and different ways of life? Can we be more inclusive of unfamiliar cultures and the expressions of them? Can we be more aware of where our food comes from and can food help bring other cultures together to better share the more common experiences of everyday life?

People bond over food and by accepting a wide range of food cultures, we can create the basis for a more diverse, inclusive society and a more civilized world. Inclusiveness can overcome indifference, if we so choose.

Oxtail Marsala ragù with buttered Cayuga Pure Organics bourbon barrel smoked cracked pepper pappardelle

3 ½ lbs of oxtails

⅓ cup to ½ cup olive oil for sautéing onions

3 medium to large yellow onions, large dice

3 large heads of garlic, cloves peeled

5 bay leaves

1 ½ Tbsp dried Sicilian wild Italian oregano

Sarawak pepper

1 750 ml. bottle Marsala wine

1 1750 gm. box Pomì brand chopped tomatoes

1 bag Cayuga Pure Organics bourbon barrel smoked cracked pepper pappardelle

7 ½ qt. enameled cast iron Dutch oven

nylon slotted spoon, chef's knife, cutting board

10-inch nonstick fry pan, silicone pasta tongs

Serve 4 to 6 people. Portion pasta accordingly. Oxtails can be made ahead and reheated.

1. Preheat oven to 350° F. Rinse 3 ½ lbs. of oxtails and add to the Dutch oven. Sear over a medium burner until browning appears on the bottom of the pot then add generous olive oil to coat the bottom.

2. Add the diced onions, the whole garlic cloves. Let stand and cook without mixing., approximately 8 to 15 minutes.

3. Stir all ingredients and add 5 fresh or dried bay leaves and the Sicilian wild Italian oregano. Stir ingredients. Crack a generous amount of Sarawak pepper over the top.

4. Cover and place in a 350° F oven to bake for 20 minutes, then remove lid to mix well and push all the bay leaves down into the onions. Increase oven heat to 450°F.

5. Cover again and bake for 10 minutes more, then turn off oven.

6. Remove from oven and pour 1 bottle of Marsala (wine) and the box of tomatoes into the pot. Stir, pushing oxtails and bay leaves down so they are covered by the liquid.

7. Cover pot and return to oven. Set timer 8 hours at 265°F. Do not leave unattended.

8. Remove from oven and skim off as much oil and fat as possible.

9. Stir ingredients and pull out bones and hard cartilage. Mix gently. Serve over butter-finished pappardelle cooked in a shallow fry pan (see below).

10. To cook pappardelle for 1 to 2 people: Fill a shallow non-stick 10-inch fry pan ¾ of the way with water and bring to a boil on high heat. Add pappardelle to fill pan almost completely. Cook, constantly pushing pasta into boiling water as it softens up, approximately 5 to 7 minutes.

11. When pasta is still a little hard, pour off ½ to ⅔ of the remaining water and reduce on high heat, constantly mixing pasta into remaining water. When about a ⅛ of an inch of water is left add a 1 ½ to 2 Tbsp of cold butter. Melt the butter and reduce to form a sauce while continually mixing with pasta tongs.

12. Or cook pasta according to packaging and stir in butter to finish. Use the suggested pasta or substitute your favorite pappardelle. Plate pasta and serve oxtail ragù over top.

Jovial, triticale & rye flour bread

400 grams bolted triticale flour

100 grams Jovial einkorn wheat flour

100 grams bolted rye flour plus dusting flour

1 1/2 cups plus 1/3 cup hot tap water

1 tsp brown sugar

1 tsp good dry baking yeast

2 tsp sea salt

1 Tbsp sunflower oil

semolina flour for dusting baking sheet

Serves 4 to 7 people.

scale that will measure in grams

two 2 qt. mixing bowls

7 qt. sturdy stainless steel mixing bowl

1/3 cup, 1/2 cup and 1 cup measures

1 tsp and 1 Tbsp measures

9 inch x 12 inch baking sheet lined with parchment paper

scissors

spray bottle with water

1. Mix the flours in the 7 qt. bowl.

2. In a 2 qt. bowl add 1 1/2 cups of hot water and the sugar, then sprinkle the yeast evenly over the surface. Add 1 cup of the flour blend and mix well. Let the yeast mixture proof for 15 minutes in a warm place. (Optional: cover with a clean kitchen towel.)

3. Add 2 tsp sea salt to remaining flour in 7 qt. bowl and mix. Make a well in the center.

4. Dust parchment-covered baking sheet with semolina flour.

5. Fill the other 2 qt. bowl most of the way with room temperature water and add 1 tsp of the yeast mixture. If it floats, it is ready. If not, continue to proof.

6. When the yeast mixture is ready, combine with the oil, then add to the well in the flour. Begin mixing, working from the center outwards until the dough forms a crumbly mix. Add a 1/3 cup hot tap water and mix until well blended.

7. Wash and dry hands, dust with rye flour, then knead and work the dough gently. Add rye flour or water as needed. Pull dough underneath itself until it holds together and forms a ball. Rub the ball with the rye dusting flour and place in the center of the semolina dusted bake sheet.

8. Loosely cover the entire baking sheet with plastic wrap. Let dough rise 45 minutes in a warm place or in the oven set at 85° to 100°F.

9. When the dough has doubled in size, remove the plastic wrap and cut an "X" in the top of the dough with scissors.

10. Spray dough with water and place the baking sheet in the oven, then turn the heat to 350°F. Bake until done, approximately 50 minutes. Spray once more with water 10 minutes before finished.

11. Let cool and serve with a good artisan butter. Bolted flours have been sifted at the mill to remove some of the bran and larger particles. Triticale is higher in protein and has a more tender gluten than wheat. Due to the lower gluten content, this tends to be a flatter Boule.

Pate Campagne

1/8 cup olive oil

1 medium sized onion in a small dice

3 large cloves of garlic chopped

1 1/2 tsp dried thyme leaf

1 1/2 lbs. raw pork liver deveined

2 tsp sea salt

1 Tbsp ground pepper

1 egg

3/4 lb. pork shoulder 3/4 inch chunks

1/2 lb. pork loin 3/4 inch chunks

6 oz. pork fatback for meat mix

5 oz. pork fatback diced for speckling

3 oz. raw pistachio optional speckling

lining for the terrine mold:
either 3/4 to 1 lb. sliced bacon or
3/4 to 1 lb fatback in one large piece

1 piece caul fat intact, carefully handled

Ice to chill terrine after cooking

chef's knife and cutting board

paring knife

10 1/2 -inch fry pan

1/8 cup measure

1 Tbsp and 1 tsp measure

Pepper mill

Kitchen scale

Mixing bowl to hold liver while slicing

terrine mold with lid (Staub, Le Creuset or other)

food processor (larger capacity)

rubber spatula

slicing knife to cut fatback leaves

medium sized deep roasting pan for cooking water bath

1 roll paper towels

aluminum foil

food-safe board and weights to press terrine in the refrigerator.

Pate Campagne

1. Heat a 10 ½-inch fry pan with ⅛ cup olive oil. Add diced onion and cook until translucent. Add garlic and thyme and cook until garlic is soft but not brown. Turn off heat and set aside.

2. Cut and tear chunks of the rinsed and dried pork liver by piercing the liver, an inch in from the edge, with the point of a sharp paring knife and tearing off 1 to 1 ½ inch chunks.

3. Place the chunks in the food processor with the onion-garlic-thyme mix plus salt and pepper.

4. Purée pork liver mix thoroughly in food processor then add the egg and purée again.

5. Add the chunks of pork shoulder and the 6 oz. of fatback to the food processor and pulse until well chopped.

6. Add pork loin and pulse ten times briefly, until just chopped; do not purée.

7. Unplug food processor and stir in diced fatback and pistachios with a rubber spatula. The forcemeat is now done.

8. Line the terrine with either strips of bacon or (butcher or hand) sliced fatback leaves. Option: line the terrine first with caul fat (crépine) by soaking it in a large bowl of cold water until it opens up in a thin membrane (see photos.)

9. Fill the terrine with the forcemeat, carefully pushing it into all corners of the mold. The terrine should be filled to the top but not spilling over.

10. Cover top of forcemeat with bacon or fatback leaves and then the optional crépine.

11. Place the lid on the terrine and refrigerate for 20 minutes to an hour to rest. If all ingredients have been kept very cold the terrine can rest overnight.

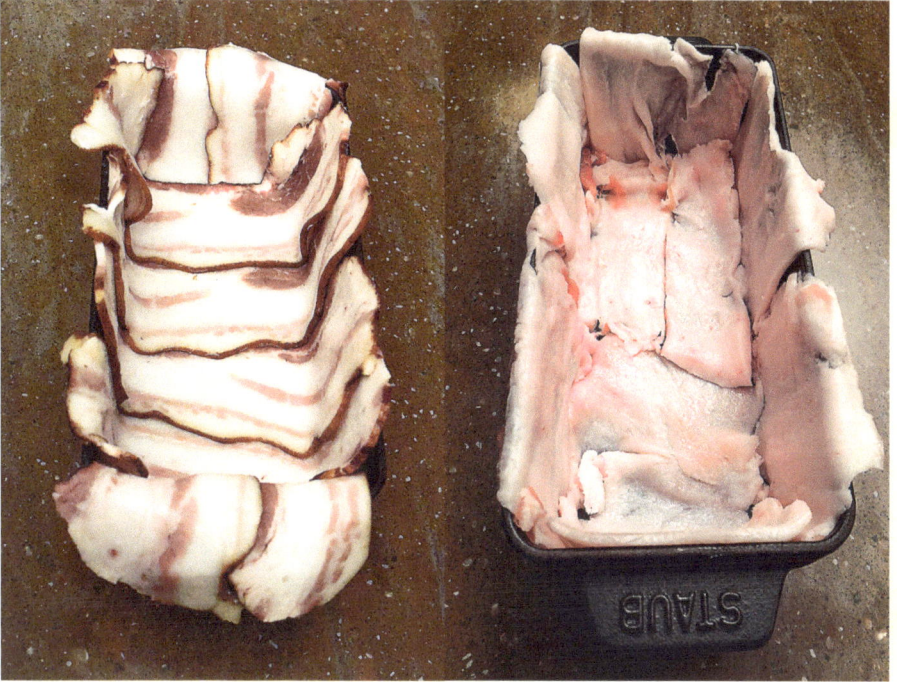

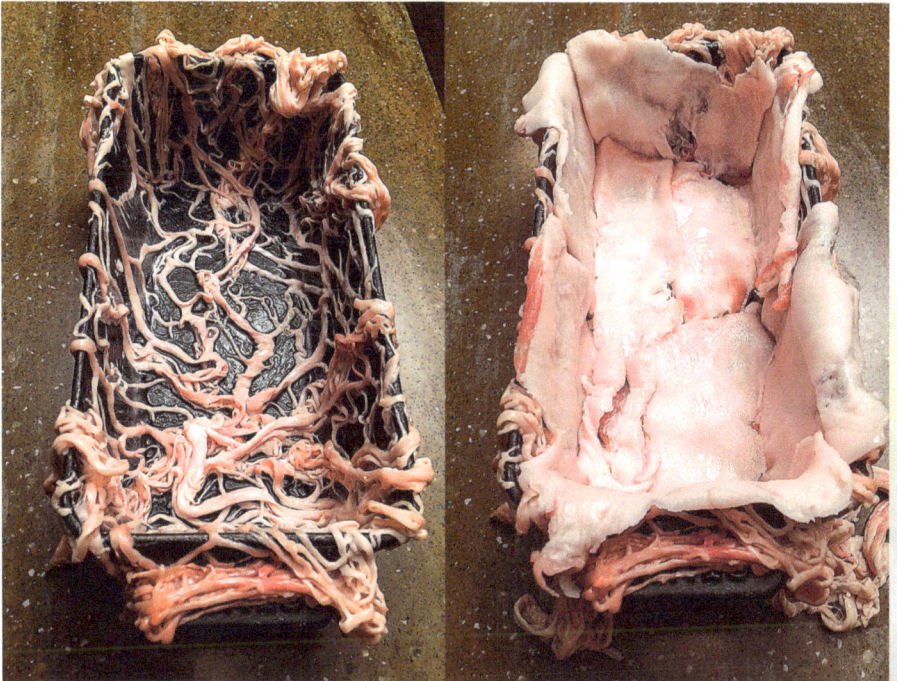

12. To cook the terrine, preheat oven to 350°F. Place the terrine in the center of the roasting pan and fill the roasting pan with boiling water as high as can be safely managed in and out of the oven. (Tip: fill the roasting pan part way then put on the oven rack. Continue to fill the roasting pan once in the oven, then close the door. Do not overflow roasting pan or terrine.)

13. Bake terrine for 1 ½ hours and shut off the oven. Leave the over door closed for one hour. (Tip: the terrine's internal temperature should be 145°F when done.)

14. Carefully remove from the oven using silicone pot holders being sure not to spill any water. (Caution: be careful, it's tricky.)

15. Pour off or scoop out water safely. When roasting pan is empty let terrine and roasting pan cool until it is safe to fill the roasting pan with ice water to cool the terrine rapidly.

16. When the terrine is cold, place it on a tray made of aluminum foil in the fridge with either a flat lid or food-safe block on top. Weight down the lid/block to press the terrine.

17. Let chill in the refrigerator overnight or up to 24 hours.

18. To unmold terrine, heat the bottom and sides of the mold in very hot water or over a gas burner. Place a block, plate or the flat lid on top of the terrine and invert it, tapping firmly to dislodge it from the mold.

19. Cover with plastic wrap, refrigerate for 2 hours until firm.

20. Slice crosswise and serve with your favorite fresh vegetable garnishes, whole grain or spicy mustard, radishes, sliced cabbage leaves or pickled vegetables.

Season

The eons spread out like the seasons before time. Soft spring was a rebirth, like the formation of the land as it came from the vastness of space to make the slow geologic migration from ice to water to earth. The seasons move forward reminiscent of the age's long slow passing. The birth of humankind was in the womb of nature's gentle mistress.

In the beginning the rains fell for millennia and the turbulent waters raced downstream as the sister named Air and brother named Earth traversed the wilderness seeking evolution. Father Sun and Mother Time emboldened Air and Earth on their quest to create the planet.

The verdant poppings and burstings of life formed eddies and the vernal pool swelled and spun in deep primordial punctuation. It whorled them into a laughing and singing that rejoiced the passing of Time's first days with Earth and Air. Father Sun majestically took his place in the order of sky and as warmer of this great land.

The growing heat of Air and Earth swirled the winds of change and the formation of climate. Soon the grasses would be tall and the fields thick with the flowers of Helios. This rite and the passing of persistent rain left Father Sun in full glory. The ruminating soil has now sprung forth its bounty and blessings of rosy pastoral.

It was the apogee of the Sun, the breadth of the Earth, the life giving of Air and the nurturing of Time that formed the world and populated it with many species of creature and the nourishment called food. Magmatic water eventually became water and nourished the land and created atmosphere. This process was as if it engulfed the family and formed what would become civilization.

Train

Wind of fall blows

The crow flies

Carpet of amber covers the field

Pale sun streaks the horizon

The chill of anticipation from movement

Family forlorn and dreaming of home

Three slats and post bound to fence

Connection of past to present

Separating self from tall milky weeds

Blister peeled and new now formed

Rail traversed

The city now in sight.

Self

Build a house with insight transparent like windows.

Create bedrock for the foundation and lay the structure brick by brick, building the house strong and tall.

Around the house plant grasses that flourish in the steady soil of well formed thought.

Steel resolve pierces the sweet skylight and draws forth the purpose.

Nourish oneself with fortitude and find the place of comfort.

Be an individual. It is the greatest gift.

Rainbow Swiss chard cakes

11 oz. rainbow Swiss chard with stems

8-inch chef's knife and cutting board

1 ½ Tbsp chopped garlic

11-inch nonstick fry pan

3/4 tsp Himala salt

silicone tongs and flat spatula

¼ cup potato flour

3 qt. mixing bowl

1 ½ Tbsp sunflower oil for frying

¼ cup, 1 Tbsp and 3/4 tsp measures

Makes about 7 cakes.

1. Thinly slice chard and stems crosswise then chop leaves lengthwise coarsely.

2. Place in a dry 11-inch nonstick fry pan and cook briefly.

3. Add garlic and salt. Cook and mix with tongs until chard wilts.

4. Transfer hot wilted chard to bowl.

5. Add potato flour all at once and mix with tongs. Work flour into chard, until well combined.

6. With hands form chard mix into 3 inch diameter by 3/4 inch thick cakes.

7. Clean fry pan, coat bottom with oil and place on medium heat.

8. Fry cakes on both sides until brown.

9. Serve hot on their own or with piment D'Espelette coulis (recipe below) and optional: raw fresh corn kernels.

Hemp milk, piment D'Espelette coulis

3/4 cup unsweetened hemp milk

8-inch nonstick fry pan

2 tsp piment D'Espelette

3/4 cup, 1 tsp and 1/8 tsp measures

1/8 tsp generous Himala salt

8-inch flat whisk

Serves 1 to 2 people.

1. In fry pan cook hemp milk, piment D'Espelette and salt over medium heat.

2. Cook until it simmers and separates

3. Let cool and recombine with whisk

4. Serve sauce room temperature or warm with swiss chard cakes.

Leaf

Maple, orange, red and yellow

Harbinger of fall

Color of new awaiting

Peace for windy presence

Sweet succulent sap in spring

Pointy high five to oncoming season

Pressed in book and swept away

Roadside painterly palate

Slippery slide on walk

Childlike amazing window wonder

First cut loose to the breezy folly

For you tell a time of change

A new being will soon unfold

Seeking warmth and comfort

For soon things will not be the same.

French toast crumpets with shredded beets, chèvre, sheep yogurt and chive

4 to 6 crumpets.	11-inch nonstick fry pan
½ cup half and half	two 2 qt. mixing bowls
2 eggs beaten	½ cup measure
1 medium beet, raw	whisk
⅓ cup chèvre	a flat spatula
⅓ cup sheep yogurt	scissors and grater
1 bunch chives, snipped	large flat plates, high rimmed
almond oil for cooking	spoons

Serves 2 to 4 people.

1. In a 2 qt. mixing bowl, add the two beaten eggs, then the half and half and mix well. Pour the egg mixture onto flat plates. On the plates, soak as many crumpets as will allow at one time. Flip over crumpets occasionally so they are well soaked on both sides. Repeat with additional crumpets as desired. Set aside.

2. Mix ⅓ cup chèvre and ⅓ cup sheep yogurt, mashing with a spoon.

3. Wash, peel and grate the beet, set aside. Snip chives with scissors, set aside.

4. Cook soaked crumpets on both sides, in an oiled frying pan, over medium heat, like French toast. Top each crumpet with a spoonful of the chèvre and yogurt mix, a smattering of beet, and a sprinkle of snipped chives.

EXQUISITE FRUIT

The color is like that of succulent sun gold tomatoes as they languish in pints brimming with honeydew like pops and snaps.

Like a brick oven huffing and puffing out crispy flat breads with bits of chorizo, purple potato and luscious tomatillo sauce.

The nectar of the corn is raw with its silk all wound around it like a summer dress wrapped in corset and husk.

These gifts from earth, sky, water and grain taste so nourishing and so sweet, oh Father harvest.

LOVE

It's gentle and supportive, like mother's milk. Love may not exist in the real world, it's all encompassing and compassionate, like a soft dream in the womb. I'm taking some license here, but I want it badly and sweetly.

TALE

The cradle's joy, free flowing and spacious, will never wither once fully taken hold.

Rabbits round the rounder bend, chasing the silliness the fox unleashes.

The raspy willow bends to break and throws back hollow holding branches, while sway lets them be strong and purposeful.

Faithful passage foreshadows the knotty clover that fortune hides behind the hallows.

Will

What is mightier than will, yet holds one powerless? It defines people and determines character or even some say, the lack of it. Will is an individual battle. It often produces the seeds to one's endeavours and catalyses the core of one's work. It can be a ten-ton load or a path to creative pursuits.

Will can create purpose in one's daily life but a much kinder way flows from even a modest use of empowerment. Wouldn't one better revel in the more playful acts of empowerment than the more work-oriented acts of will? Can more progress be made when the resistance is reduced and doing becomes an act of joy?

Can one find the joy in food and the act of eating responsibly? If so, isn't this of more service to oneself? Isn't embracing the pleasure of food a better path to a healthy diet and good nutrition? This can make eating responsibly seem possible and puts the path to a heathy lifestyle within reach.

NO SINGLE FOOD WILL MAKE YOU HEALTHY, SAVE YOUR LIFE OR CREATE BALANCE.

Eat a clean, well balanced diet of nothing but what comes straight out of the ground or of this earth, without anything added or modified, and you will be on the road to good health and a better chance at life.

Song

As I lie in bed, I sleep, I wake.
As dreams unfold, the earth I take.
Awake the Spring and Summer make.
In the Fall and Winter a rest I partake.
Growth to me the seasons bring
and the harvest of what sweetly sings.

www.ingramcontent.com/pod-product-compliance
Lightning Source LLC
Chambersburg PA
CBHW041957090426

42811CB00014B/1528